Firestone
Success Begins Here

Macbeth
25 Key Quotations for GCSE
Dan Smith

Series Editor: Hannah Rabey

firestonebooks.com

Macbeth
25 Key Quotations for GCSE
Dan Smith

Series Editor: Hannah Rabey

Text © Dan Smith
About this Book section © Hannah Rabey

Cover © XL Book Cover Design
xlbookcoverdesign.co.uk

2021 Edition

ISBN-13: 9798670574198

Published by Firestone Books

The right of Dan Smith to be identified as the author of this work has been asserted by her in accordance with the Copyright, Designs and Patents Act 1988

All rights reserved. This publication may not be reproduced or transmitted in any form or by any means, electronic, mechanical, photocopying, recording or otherwise without prior permission from Firestone Books.

This guide is not endorsed by or affiliated with any exam boards/awarding bodies.

firestonebooks.com

You can stay up to date by following Firestone Books on Facebook and Twitter, or subscribing to our fabulous newsletter.
Go on – you know you want to…

Contents

About this Book	5
A Biography of William Shakespeare	6
A Chronology of the Quotations in this Guide	9
A Summary of the Key Events in *Macbeth*	11
Macbeth: 25 Key Quotations for GCSE	**15**
Glossary of Key Terms	66

About this Book

The GCSE English Literature exam relies on understanding a wide range of relevant references, studied both in lessons and as part of revision. This guide will provide you with in-depth analysis of 25 key quotations in William Shakespeare's play *Macbeth*, written by experts to ensure that you are prepared for success.

In this guide you will find:

- A biography of William Shakespeare's life
- A chronology of the quotations throughout the play
- A summary of the key events in *Macbeth*
- 25 key analysed quotations
- A key terms glossary

The 25 quotations include:

- Detailed analysis of the quotation
- Key context relating to the quotation
- A list of key themes and characters that the quotation links to (key terms are denoted by an asterisk)

A Biography of William Shakespeare

Born in Stratford-upon-Avon, William Shakespeare was the son of John Shakespeare, a successful glove-maker, and Mary Arden, the daughter of a prosperous farmer. Shakespeare's date of birth is unknown but he was baptised, most likely within a few days of his birth, on 26th April 1564.

At the age of eighteen he married Anne Hathaway who was eight years his senior. Six months later, in May 1583, Anne gave birth to a daughter, Susanna, and in 1585 Anne also gave birth to twins, Hamnet and Judith.

Between 1585 and 1592 almost nothing is known of Shakespeare's life, the so called "lost years". Many apocryphal tales about this period have been reported including that he fled his hometown for London to escape prosecution for deer poaching, that he started his theatrical career minding the horses of wealthy theatregoers, and that he may have been briefly employed as a schoolmaster in Lancashire.

By 1592 Shakespeare was an established playwright, with several of his plays having been staged in London. It is also the year that fellow playwright, Robert Greene, published his infamous *Groats-Worth of Wit* in which he attacked Shakespeare for trying to match the writing of university educated writers such as Christopher Marlowe and Thomas Nashe.

Shakespeare's plays were only performed by the Lord Chamberlain's Men, a company of actors in which Shakespeare had a share. In 1599 some members of the Lord Chamberlain's Men built their own theatre on the south bank of the river Thames and named it *The Globe*. As a shareholder in this theatre, holding up to 3000 spectators, Shakespeare became a wealthy man.

Prior to 1599 Shakespeare had only written two tragedies: *Titus Andronicus* and *Romeo and Juliet*, with his focus being more on comedies, history plays and poems. After 1599 he almost stopped writing history plays and instead switched to writing tragedies, writing many of his finest plays including: *Hamlet, Othello, King Lear* and *Macbeth.*

In 1603 the new King, James I, awarded the Lord Chamberlain's Men a royal patent and the company changed its name to the King's Men.

As well as writing plays, Shakespeare also wrote two long poems and a collection of sonnets. The sonnets describe two love affairs, but who these lovers were – or even if they were real or imagined – remains a mystery.

As Shakespeare was also an actor, it meant that rather than working on his plays in isolation he would have worked closely with other actors. Many of the plots for the plays came from history books, or earlier Italian tales, so it is difficult, if not impossible, to work out which contributions were Shakespeare's. Even when he'd finished a particular play, it was still likely to be re-worked by actors and others – something that is done to this day, and keeps his work as fresh and interesting as it has ever been.

Though Shakespeare worked as a writer and actor in London for most of his adult life, his did spend much of his time in Stratford-upon-Avon where, in 1597, he bought New Place as his family home. It's known that Shakespeare was still working as an actor in London in 1608, and that he also retired to Stratford 'some years before his death'.

Shakespeare died on the 23rd of April 1616, around the time of his 52nd birthday. It was said by John Ward, the vicar of Stratford, writing in the mid-1600s that 'Shakespeare, Drayton and Ben Johnson had a merry meeting and, it seems, drank too hard, for Shakespeare died of a fever there contracted.'

Shakespeare was buried at the Holy Trinity Church – the place of his baptism over half a century earlier. The epitaph on his gravestone has a curse against disturbing his resting place:

> *Good friend, for Jesus' sake forbear,*
> *To dig the dust enclosed here.*
> *Blessed be the man that spares these stones,*
> *And cursed be he that moves my bones.*

Fellow dramatist, Ben Johnson, famously and presciently referred to Shakespeare as being 'not of an age, but for all time'. Since his death Shakespeare's reputation has grown, leading him to now be widely regarded as the greatest writer in the English language and the world's greatest dramatist.

A Chronology of the Quotations in this Guide

Quotation 1: "Fair is foul and foul is fair / Hover through the fog and filthy air" (Act 1, Scene 1)

Quotation 2: "…his brandish'd steel, / Which smoked with bloody execution / Like valour's minion carved out his passage" (Act 1, Scene 2)

Quotation 3: "As sparrows eagles, or the hare the lion / …As cannons overcharged with double cracks" (Act 1, Scene 2)

Quotation 4: "So foul and fair a day I have not seen." (Act 1, Scene 3)

Quotation 5: "If you can look into the seeds of time, / And say which grain will grow and which will not" (Act 1, Scene 3)

Quotation 6: "Stars, hide your fires; / Let not light see my black and deep desires" (Act 1, Scene 4)

Quotation 7: "yet I do fear thy nature / It is too full o' th' milk of human kindness / to catch the nearest way" (Act 1, Scene 5)

Quotation 8: "…look like the innocent flower / But be the serpent under't" (Act 1, Scene 5)

Quotation 9: "He's here in double trust; / First, as I am his kinsman and his subject, / Strong both against the deed; then, as his host, / Who should against his murderer shut the door, / Not bear the knife myself." (Act 1, Scene 7)

Quotation 10: "What beast was't, then, / That made you break this enterprise to me?" (Act 1, Scene 7)

Quotation 11: "Art thou but / A dagger of the mind, a false creation?" (Act 2, Scene 1)

Quotation 12: "Will all great Neptune's ocean wash this blood / Clean from my hand? No, this my hand will rather / The multitudinous seas incarnadine, / Making the green one red." (Act 2, Scene 2)

Quotation 13: "My hands are of your colour; but I shame / To wear a heart so white." (Act 2, Scene 2)

Quotation 14: "'Tis unnatural...On Tuesday last, / A falcon, towering in her pride of place, / Was by a mousing owl hawk'd at and kill'd" (Act 2, Scene 4)

Quotation 15: "I fear, / Thou play'dst most foully for't:" (Act 3, Scene 1)

Quotation 16: "O, full of scorpions is my mind, dear wife!" (Act 3, Scene 2)

Quotation 17: "Thou canst not say I did it: never shake / Thy gory locks at me" (Act 3, Scene 4)

Quotation 18: "By the pricking of my thumbs, / Something wicked this way comes." (Act 4, Scene 1)

Quotation 19: "Be bloody, bold, and resolute; laugh to scorn / The power of man, for none of woman born / Shall harm Macbeth." (Act 4, Scene 1)

Quotation 20: "He has no children. All my pretty ones? / Did you say all? O hell-kite! All? / What, all my pretty chickens and their dam / At one fell swoop?" (Act 4, Scene 3)

Quotation 21: "Out, damned spot! out, I say! - One: two: why, / then, 'tis time to do't. - Hell is murky!" (Act 5, Scene 1)

Quotation 22: "Here's the smell of the blood still: all the / perfumes of Arabia will not sweeten this little / hand. Oh, oh, oh!" (Act 5, Scene 1)

Quotation 23: "Turn, hell-hound, turn!" (Act 5, Scene 8)

Quotation 24: "Despair thy charm; / And let the angel whom thou still hast served / Tell thee, Macduff was from his mother's womb / Untimely ripp'd." (Act 5, Scene 8)

Quotation 25: "Of this dead butcher and his fiend-like queen" (Act 5, Scene 8)

A Summary of the Key Events in *Macbeth*

The play is set in Scotland and opens with the three Witches on stage, who seem to be casting a spell. The opening to *Macbeth* sets an evil and ominous tone. We then meet the good King Duncan at his military camp, who is at war with both invading forces and with traitors within Scotland. King Duncan is told by one of his officers that two Thanes*, Macbeth and Banquo, have helped to win key battles by leading ruthless charges and killing one of the traitors. For his bravery in leading the charge, King Duncan wants to reward Macbeth, who is already the Thane of Glamis, by making him the Thane of Cawdor. The current Thane of Cawdor is one of the traitors, who has been captured and sentenced to death. King Duncan sends a messenger to give Macbeth the good news.

On their way back from the battlefield, Macbeth and Banquo meet the three Witches. The Witches tell Macbeth that he is Thane of Glamis, Thane of Cawdor and he will become King of Scotland. Macbeth appears stunned by the Witches, but Banquo demands to know what he has in his future. The Witches tell Banquo that he will not be king, but that his children and descendants will form a line of kings.

The Witches vanish, leaving Macbeth and Banquo to wonder about the truth and possible impact of the prophecies. King Duncan's messenger then arrives and confirms that Macbeth is now the Thane of Cawdor. The Witches have now been proved right and this causes Macbeth to wonder about becoming King and how that could be possible.

Macbeth and Banquo join King Duncan and the other Thanes at the camp. King Duncan compliments Macbeth and Banquo on their actions in battle, but then names Malcolm, King Duncan's first born, as the next in line to the throne. Malcolm is now in the way of Macbeth becoming King and this causes further confusion and conflict in Macbeth's mind. King Duncan announces that he will be staying at Macbeth's castle that evening and Macbeth sends a letter to his wife, Lady Macbeth, explaining everything that has happened so far.

After reading the letter, Lady Macbeth is determined that Macbeth should kill King Duncan that night. Lady Macbeth calls upon evil forces to make her less feminine, so that she is strong to go through with the murder and to not feel guilty about it afterwards. When Macbeth arrives home, Lady Macbeth is very manipulative and gets Macbeth to agree to killing King Duncan.

Lady Macbeth's plan is to get King Duncan's guards so drunk that they pass out; Macbeth can then sneak in and kill the King with the guards' own daggers. Macbeth will then leave the daggers by the servants and smear Duncan's blood on the guards' clothes, framing them.

The thought of murdering the King is deeply troubling for Macbeth for many reasons and he questions it many times. The idea of the murder also makes Macbeth see a dagger that turns bloody. Macbeth does go ahead with killing King Duncan, however he is so upset and disturbed by what he has done that he forgets to frame the guards. When Lady Macbeth sees Macbeth with the daggers, she orders him to go back, but he refuses, forcing her to frame the guards herself.

When Duncan's body is discovered the next day, Macbeth kills the guards immediately, claiming that he could not control his anger. Duncan's two sons, Malcolm and Donalbain, decide that they must leave Scotland or risk being killed next. Malcolm leaves for England and Donalbain for Ireland. As the two sons have run away, they become suspects in their father's murder and Macbeth is crowned King of Scotland.

The Witches' prophecies cause Macbeth and Banquo to be suspicious of each other. Before Banquo can escape with his son

Fleance, Macbeth hires a group of murderers to ambush and kill them both. Banquo is killed in the ambush but Fleance escapes. One of the murderers reports back to Macbeth about the violent death of Banquo and that Fleance is still alive. Macbeth worries about Fleance becoming a threat in the future.

At the feast the same evening, Macbeth sees Banquo's ghost and starts ranting and raving at it. None of the other characters can see the ghost and they are deeply alarmed by Macbeth's behaviour. Lady Macbeth tries to calm the guests and Macbeth, but she fails.

Macbeth goes to the Witches to demand answers. The Witches show Macbeth a series of apparitions or visions that present him with further prophecies: Macbeth must beware Macduff, the Thane of Fife; Macbeth cannot be killed by any man born of woman and he will not be defeated until Birnam Wood comes to Dunsinane Castle. Macbeth feels relieved because he thinks that the prophecies mean that he is invincible, as all men are born of women and trees cannot move of their own accord. When Macbeth hears that Macduff has gone to England to meet with Malcolm, Macbeth orders the slaughter of Lady Macduff and their children. Macduff is told about the death of his family during his meeting with Malcolm in England and swears revenge against Macbeth.

Malcolm has raised a large army in England and Macduff joins him as he marches the army up to Scotland. The army has the support of all the Thanes of Scotland, who are disgusted by Macbeth's murderous behaviour.

Lady Macbeth has now been overcome with guilt, not only for her part in the murder of King Duncan, but also for all the killing that Macbeth has gone on to commit. Lady Macbeth sleepwalks and complains of bloodstains she cannot remove. In the middle of preparing for battle, Macbeth is told that Lady Macbeth has died, 'thought, by self and violent hands', causing him to grimly reflect on life and death. Macbeth's belief that he cannot be killed is then shaken when he learns that the English Army is carrying branches of the trees from Birnam Wood; the wood is coming to Dunsinane.

In the final battle, Macbeth fights ruthlessly, but the English forces are at an advantage due to their numbers and because many of Macbeth's soldiers do not really want to fight for him. Macduff confronts Macbeth on the battlefield; when Macbeth warns Macduff that none of woman born can harm him, Macduff responds that he was 'ripped' from his mother's womb, what we might call a caesarean section. Macbeth realises that he has been tricked by the prophecies and he is killed by Macduff. Malcolm is named the King of Scotland and he gives a speech calling an end to the bloodshed caused by Macbeth and Lady Macbeth.

Macbeth

25 Key Quotations for GCSE

Quotation 1

Act 1, Scene 1

The Witches:
"Fair is foul and foul is fair / Hover through the fog and filthy air."

Characters: The Witches, Macbeth

Analysis: The Witches wish to reverse the 'natural' order of the world, making what is good into evil and making evil a virtue. Several characters in the play, including the original Thane* of Cawdor, Lady Macbeth and Macbeth, were loyal and 'fair' at first, before turning 'foul' or evil. The alliteration* of the 'f' sound adds to the ominous tone and the juxtaposition* of 'fair' and 'foul' emphasises the Witches' desire to replace good with evil. The 'fog' also creates poor visibility, which could also metaphorically* imply that the Witches will destroy Macbeth's ability to view anything clearly and rationally. The 'filthy air' suggests that the presence of the Witches and the trouble they will cause pollutes the environment for the other characters.

Context: The belief in witchcraft was widespread when *Macbeth* was first performed in 1606. Even the monarch at the time, King James VI and I (1566-1625), wrote about the supernatural* and his experience with witches in works such as *Daemonologie*, which first appeared in Scotland in 1597. Whilst his views eventually became more sceptical, the king influenced perceptions of witchcraft and he personally oversaw the trial of witches. Large numbers of people, particularly women, across the world were accused of being witches and were consequently killed during this period. Jacobean* audiences would therefore have understood the dangerous role the witches played in *Macbeth* and the fear that their presence would have created.

Themes: Appearance versus reality, good versus evil, the supernatural

Techniques: Alliteration, juxtaposition of 'foul' and 'fair', repetition*

Structure: The Witches speak in a different rhythm or meter to the rest of the characters in the play. The rhythm or meter is a modified form of trochaic tetrameter*. The Witches also open the play, and the sense of pathetic fallacy created through the 'fog' and filthy air' immediately sets a dark and ominous tone.

Using this quotation: This quotation establishes a sense of foreboding and corruption at the beginning of the play so can be used when discussing the influence of evil and the Witches.

Links in the text: Macbeth, "So foul and fair a day I have not seen" (Act 1, Scene 3).

Questions to consider:
- How would you feel watching this moment if you lived in the 1600s?
- How important do you think the Witches are to the play?

Quotation 2

Act 1, Scene 2

Sergeant:

"…his brandish'd steel, / Which smoked with bloody execution / Like valour's minion carved out his passage"

Characters: Sergeant, referring to Macbeth

Analysis: The Sergeant describes Macbeth's sword as 'smoking' or steaming with 'bloody execution'. This metaphor* illustrates the speed at which Macbeth's sword is moving. Moreover, the image of steam could also represent the warm blood that covers the sword, radiating heat across the freezing battlefield. Macbeth is described as a 'minion' of 'valour', or the servant or messenger of bravery itself, which is ironic* due to his cowardly behaviour later in the play. The verb 'carved' emphasises the ruthless and bloody way that Macbeth kills the enemy.

Context: The concept of honour and bravery were very important in the eleventh century (when *Macbeth* is set). At the beginning of the play, Macbeth represents the perfect soldier and hero, as seen in his bravery and skill in battle. The Sergeant reports to King Duncan that a crucial* battle has been won due to the actions of Macbeth, supported by Banquo. The Sergeant explains that Macbeth expertly swung his sword, killing so many enemy soldiers that his sword was covered in blood, until he found and killed the traitorous Macdonwald. This betrayal foreshadows Macbeth's own treachery. After Macdonwald's death the title of Thane of Cawdor is passed on to Macbeth who betrays King Duncan.

Themes: Blood, bravery, violence, war

Techniques: Foreshadowing, metaphor, personification*

Structure: The Sergeant speaks in iambic pentameter*. This rhythm or meter is appropriate* because of his rank, the topic of conversation and because he is addressing the King. However, the line beginning 'Which smoked…' is only nine syllables. As this line ends on the word 'execution', it could be suggested that the Sergeant emphasises Macbeth's role as 'executioner', shortening the lives of enemy soldiers.

Using this quotation: This quotation demonstrates Macbeth's violent and ruthless nature and can also be used for themes of violence and for the importance of blood in the play.

Links in the text: There are over 40 references to blood in *Macbeth*; links can be made to the 'bloody execution' of King Duncan, the framing of the guards, Duncan and Banquo's 'bloodline' and blood on Macbeth and Lady Macbeth's hands as a symbol of guilt.

Questions to consider:
- How powerful, and possibly dangerous, does the Sergeant make Macbeth sound?
- Why is Banquo not described in the same way?

Quotation 3

Act 1, Scene 2

Sergeant:
"As sparrows eagles, or the hare the lion / ...As cannons overcharged with double cracks."

Characters: Sergeant, referring to Macbeth and Banquo

Analysis: The Sergeant ironically states that Macbeth and Banquo were as scared of the enemy as eagles would be of sparrows, or lions would be of hares (rabbits). This use of animal imagery is used throughout the play. Macbeth and Banquo are also described by the Sergeant as 'cannons overcharged with double cracks', meaning that Macbeth and Banquo have the frightening power of cannons loaded with double charges of gunpowder. This could also be a warning as 'overcharged' suggests a lack of control and further in the passage, the Captain asks why they fought so hard 'Except they meant to bathe in reeking wounds', meaning that they wanted to create complete terror and destruction on the battleground. This therefore hints at Macbeth's future instability and the blood he and Lady Macbeth would imagine they were covered with.

Context: The Sergeant reports to King Duncan that a crucial battle has been won due to the actions of Macbeth and Banquo. The

King asks the Sergeant whether Macbeth or Banquo were 'dismayed' or scared by a fresh wave of attacks and the Sergeant uses irony* to explain that the two men were not frightened, but instead were very brave.

Themes: Bravery, nature, violence, war

Techniques: Irony, simile*

Structure: The Sergeant is speaking in iambic pentameter; this rhythm or meter is appropriate because of his rank, the topic of conversation and because he is addressing King Duncan.

Using this quotation: This quotation can be used in an exam question about Macbeth, Banquo and the themes of violence and nature.

Links in the text: In Act 2, Scene 4 the Old Man states "A falcon, towering in her pride of place, / Was by a mousing owl hawk'd at and kill'd".

Questions to consider:
- How powerful, and possibly dangerous, does the Sergeant make Macbeth sound?
- What other animal metaphors can you think of in the play?

Quotation 4

Act 1, Scene 3

Macbeth:
"So foul and fair a day I have not seen."

Characters: Macbeth

Analysis: Macbeth is describing the day that he and Banquo have just experienced. Macbeth contrasts 'foul' and 'fair' for a range of reasons. Firstly, the battle has been won for King Duncan, but it was very difficult and bloody; without the intervention of Macbeth, supported by Banquo, the battle could have been lost. Secondly, the battle has been won, however it involved killing several traitors who were once trusted brothers in arms. Macbeth could also be referring to winning a battle in awful, ominous weather. Most importantly, Macbeth's first line reflects the language of the Witches. Macbeth's use of 'foul' and 'fair' could reveal a couple of intentions by Shakespeare. Firstly, Macbeth's use of similar language to the Witches could convey that the atmosphere* of Scotland has already started to become affected by the spell cast by the Witches in the first scene. Furthermore, the similar use of language could also suggest that Macbeth is also starting to come under the influence of the Witches.

Context: This is the first line spoken by Macbeth, after the difficult victory against the invaders and traitors to the King.

Themes: The supernatural, violence

Techniques: Juxtaposition, metaphor

Structure: Iambic pentameter, unlike the modified form of trochaic tetrameter that the Witches use when they first mention 'foul' and 'fair'.

Using this quotation: This quotation is very useful for the beginning of Macbeth's character arc* and it is also useful in a question about the Witches' influence on Macbeth, as seen in Act 1, Scene 1.

Links in the text: Consider the parallels between the Witches' language and Macbeth's language throughout the play.

Questions to consider:
- How does Shakespeare gradually shift Macbeth's vocabulary throughout the play?

Quotation 5

Act 1, Scene 3

Banquo:

"If you can look into the seeds of time, / And say which grain will grow and which will not"

Characters: Banquo, speaking to the Witches and referencing Macbeth

Analysis: Banquo is questioning whether the Witches can actually see the future, whether they can predict which 'seeds' will grow and which will not. Shakespeare is referencing the Bible, specifically Ecclesiastes 11.6, which says 'thou knowest not' which seed 'shall prosper'. Unlike Macbeth, Banquo is suspicious and questioning of the Witches and their intentions. He has the rational logic that Macbeth does not possess. This is one reference to the motif of time which is used throughout the play to count down to Macbeth's downfall and the rightful King, Malcolm, taking the throne at the end of the play.

Context: Macbeth and Banquo have encountered the Witches who have just told Macbeth that he is Thane of Cawdor and will become King. Banquo is both sceptical of the Witches' powers and is also perhaps frustrated that the Witches have not yet spoken to him.

By the sixteenth century the preternatural* was a popular term to describe things not seen to be normal, natural or Godly, such as the demonic and the deception and trickery of witches. Many people were very cautious and superstitious of the preternatural, and Banquo is used to represent these ideas when he challenges the Witches' prophecies and influence over Macbeth.

Themes: Macbeth and Banquo's relationship, kingship, the preternatural, the supernatural

Techniques: Biblical* imagery, metaphor, motif

Structure: Banquo speaks in iambic pentameter, which is appropriate to his status. It could also be argued that Banquo is speaking in a commanding tone to the Witches.

Using this quotation: This quotation could be used in an exam question on the supernatural, but perhaps more importantly on the relationship between Macbeth and Banquo, as it begins to hint at the growing tension between them.

Links in the text: In Act 3, Scene 1, Banquo's opening soliloquy* explores his suspicions that Macbeth 'played most foully' for the crown. Banquo also considers whether the Witches are his 'oracles' as well. The Witches also give Macbeth further prophecies in Act 4, Scene 1 that give him a false sense of security.

Questions to consider:
- Would Macbeth have become King if he had not spoken to the Witches?
- How do Macbeth and Banquo react differently to the Witches?

Quotation 6

Act 1, Scene 4

Macbeth:

"Stars, hide your fires; / Let not light see my black and deep desires"

Characters: Macbeth

Analysis: Macbeth tells heaven or the 'stars' to not look at, or expose, the darkness inside him, using the metaphor 'hide your fires'. The juxtaposition of 'light' and 'black' represents good and evil. The alliteration 'deep desires' conveys how Macbeth's ambition* to become king was buried within him, and that it also has a powerful or 'deep' pull.

Context: King Duncan has officially named his son, Malcolm, as next in line to the throne. Macbeth now knows that if he wants to become king, he must kill King Duncan and possibly Malcolm as well. Macbeth's murderous thoughts are dangerous and even frightening to him. Although at the beginning of the play Macbeth appears to be a great hero, by this point in Act 1 he starts to fulfil the Greek philosopher Aristotle's criteria of the tragic hero, which include:

- **Hamartia:** a tragic flaw that causes the downfall of the hero – in Macbeth's case, ambition.

- **Hubris:** excessive pride and disrespect for the natural order of the world – seen through Macbeth's reliance on the Witches and his disregard for the divine right of kings*.
- **Peripeteia:** the tragic hero's realisation that what he believes in is wrong, often leading to overwhelming emotions. One example of this is when Macbeth worries about the murders of Banquo and Fleance, and states "I am in blood / Stepp'd in so far, that, should I wade no more, / Returning were as tedious as go o'er" in Act 3, Scene 4.
- **Anagnorisis:** a moment when the tragic hero makes an important discovery. A key moment is when Macbeth realises that he has been tricked by the Witches' prophecies in Act 5.
- **Nemesis:** a punishment that the tragic hero cannot avoid, usually occurring as a result of his hubris, in Macbeth's case, his execution due to the murders he is responsible for.
- **Catharsis:** the releasing of strong emotions by the audience, as seen through the audience's pity of Macbeth when his downfall leads him to state of his life in Act 5 "a poor player / That struts and frets his hour upon the stage / And then is heard no more… Signifying nothing."

Themes: Ambition, foreshadowing, good versus evil

Techniques: Alliteration, juxtaposition, metaphor

Structure: Iambic pentameter

Using this quotation: This quotation is central to demonstrating Macbeth's inner struggle between his conscience and his ambition that will lead him to killing King Duncan.

Links in the text: This quotation links to Macbeth's later soliloquy when he argues with himself about killing King Duncan and arguably links to Macbeth's later 'black' or dark actions.

Questions to consider:
- How does Shakespeare foreshadow Macbeth's descent into violent tyranny?

Quotation 7

Act 1, Scene 5

Lady Macbeth:
"yet I do fear thy nature / It is too full o' th' milk of human kindness / to catch the nearest way"

Characters: Lady Macbeth, describing Macbeth

Analysis: The 'nearest way' is a euphemism* for murdering the King; interestingly, Macbeth and Lady Macbeth do not use the phrase 'murder the King' or 'kill the King', perhaps because of the enormity of the deed. The metaphor 'milk of human kindness' illustrates that Macbeth may not be able to go through with the murder, as he is too kind and humane for it. The use of 'milk' could symbolise typically maternal qualities of caring and nurturing, which Lady Macbeth insults. The audience is informed that the Macbeths have lost a child so Lady Macbeth perhaps feels she has failed to provide her husband with an heir, which was a crucial requirement of being a wife at the time, and so she criticises any sort of maternal qualities. Secondly, this is an example of Lady Macbeth's use of emasculation* to control Macbeth. By stating that he is maternal, rather than brave and warrior-like, she manipulates him into killing King Duncan.

Context: Lady Macbeth has just read Macbeth's letter explaining his encounter with the Witches and their prophecy that he will become king. Lady Macbeth is very excited by this, but she is worried that, although Macbeth is a brave and ruthless warrior on the battlefield, he is too kind and humane to commit murder.

As this play was written and performed shortly after the discovery of the Gunpowder Plot on 5 November 1605, a plot which aimed to assassinate King James, the audience would have been fully aware of the severity of such a crime.

Themes: Ambition, gender roles, good and evil, the relationship between Lady Macbeth and Macbeth, the supernatural

Techniques: Euphemism, metaphor

Structure: This quotation is part of a soliloquy that opens Act 1, Scene 5. It is composed* in iambic pentameter, however the line beginning 'it is too full...' has more than ten syllables which could emphasise Macbeth being 'too full' of kindness.

Using this quotation: This quotation could be used in a question about the manipulation of Macbeth by Lady Macbeth and her strength as a woman in comparison to her husband.

Links in the text: In the same scene, Lady Macbeth ask 'murdering ministers', meaning demons or spirits, 'to take her milk for gall'. Lady Macbeth wants her maternal, kind, gentle nature taken away and replaced by 'gall' or poison.

Questions to consider:
- How does Shakespeare demonstrate Lady Macbeth's dominance in the relationship between her and Macbeth?

Quotation 8

Act 1, Scene 5

Lady Macbeth:
"...look like the innocent flower / But be the serpent under't"

Characters: Lady Macbeth, talking to Macbeth

Analysis: The simile of the 'flower' illustrates that Macbeth should appear to be friendly and harmless. However, the metaphor of the 'serpent' demonstrates that Macbeth will betray the king. The progression of the simile to the metaphor conveys that Macbeth's harmless appearance is false and his true intent is to kill the King.

Context: Lady Macbeth is concerned that Macbeth's emotions and thoughts show too easily on his face; Macbeth is an 'open book' and he needs to hide his true emotions.

Additionally, the image of the serpent among the flowers is significant for two main reasons. Firstly, the serpent references the devil as the serpent in the Garden of Eden, hiding among the branches of the tree of the knowledge of good and evil. In Genesis, Adam and Eve were tempted to eat the forbidden fruit on the tree by the serpent. This is known as the Fall of Man in Christianity as Adam and Eve turn from Godly obedience to guilty disobedience, corrupting the world and causing great suffering. God states in

Genesis 2:17, 'But from the tree of the knowledge of good and evil you shall not eat, for in the day that you eat from it you shall surely die'. In *Macbeth* the temptations the Witches offer, like the serpent, lead to the deaths of Macbeth and Lady Macbeth. Their ambition – their hamartia and hubris – creates great evil and temporarily destroys good and order in Scotland. This was arguably a warning by Shakespeare to those who wished to go against God and the natural order of the world.

Secondly, King James commissioned* a medal after the Gunpowder Plot was discovered and foiled*; the medal depicts a serpent hiding among flowers and a Jacobean audience would have recognised this allusion.

Themes: Allusion, ambition, appearance versus reality, evil

Techniques: Biblical reference, metaphor*, simile

Structure: Iambic pentameter

Using this quotation: This quotation can be used in a question about the evil deeds of Lady Macbeth and Macbeth, and the dangers of appearance versus reality.

Links in the text: Macbeth echoes the language used by Lady Macbeth in Act 1, Scene 7, stating "False face must hide what the false heart doth know". Macbeth also echoes this language in Act 3, Scene 2: "make our faces vizards (masks) to our hearts", in order to successfully have Banquo murdered.

Questions to consider:
- How important is the Gunpowder plot as context* for *Macbeth*?
- How are Biblical references used by Shakespeare in *Macbeth*?

Quotation 9

Act 1, Scene 7

Macbeth:
"He's here in double trust; / First, as I am his kinsman and his subject, / Strong both against the deed; then, as his host, / Who should against his murderer shut the door, / Not bear the knife myself."

Characters: Macbeth, referring to King Duncan

Analysis: Macbeth states that King Duncan is staying at the castle in 'double trust' which means that Duncan has two very powerful reasons to believe he is safe: firstly, as Duncan's 'kinsman and subject' Macbeth should have unwavering loyalty to Duncan and be completely in Duncan's service. Secondly, as a 'host', Macbeth should consider it his duty to protect and care for King Duncan as his guest. If Macbeth goes ahead, not only is he not protecting his guest, he is 'bearing the knife himself'. These metaphors not only refer to the physical act of killing the King, but also to the murderous thoughts, which he should 'shut the door' on.

Context: Lady Macbeth has told Macbeth that they must take advantage of King Duncan staying with them and kill him before he leaves the next morning. Macbeth is deeply conflicted about this.

By murdering the King, Macbeth acts against the divine right of kings, a system based on kings being chosen by God, and gaining their authority and power through Him. A king's actions were held accountable by God and not humanity. King James was a strong believer in the divine right of kings. When Macbeth ignores this system, an audience at the time would have seen this as a challenge to God's authority.

Themes: Loyalty, violence, right versus wrong

Techniques: Metaphor

Structure: A soliloquy in iambic pentameter

Using this quotation: This quotation can be used in a question about Macbeth, King Duncan, loyalty, and good versus evil.

Links in the text: Macbeth's conflicted and disturbing thoughts are referenced just before he murders the king when he hallucinates seeing a dagger in Act 2, Scene 1.

Questions to consider:
- What other arguments does Macbeth use against killing the king in Act 1, Scene 7?
- Why does Shakespeare create a character that challenges the divine right of kings?

Quotation 10

Act 1, Scene 7

Lady Macbeth:
"What beast was't, then, / That made you break this enterprise to me?"

Characters: Lady Macbeth, talking to Macbeth

Analysis: Lady Macbeth is questioning whether Macbeth is really a 'man'. Lady Macbeth is claiming that Macbeth is breaking a promise and is doing so because of cowardice. A man in this time period would be expected to keep his promises or oaths, and to be brave. Instead of calling Macbeth a man, Lady Macbeth calls him a 'beast' that has broken a promise, or 'breaking' the 'enterprise'. The rhetorical question* is a challenge to Macbeth and conveys Lady Macbeth's dominant position in the relationship at this moment in the play. Ironically, Lady Macbeth goes on to display her animalistic and beastly tendencies when she states that "I have given suck, and know / How tender 'tis to love the babe that milks me: / I would, while it was smiling in my face, / Have pluck'd my nipple from his boneless gums, / And dash'd the brains out, had I so sworn as you / Have done to this." The juxtaposition of the maternal imagery and innocence symbolised by babies with Lady Macbeth's murderous capacity both demonstrate her lack of maternalism but also the value that promises hold for her.

Context: Macbeth is trying to put a stop to the plan to kill King Duncan; Lady Macbeth is furious and confronts Macbeth.

Themes: Ambition, guilt

Techniques: Metaphor, rhetorical question*

Structure: Iambic pentameter

Using this quotation: This quotation can be used for Macbeth, Lady Macbeth and the relationship between them. It is an example of Lady Macbeth's continuous emasculation of her husband and her disgust with his inability to be what she sees as a 'man'.

Links in the text: Compare Lady Macbeth's dominant position with Macbeth's dominant position in Act 3.

Questions to consider:
- How does Shakespeare portray the changes in the balance of power between Macbeth and Lady Macbeth?

Quotation 11

Act 2, Scene 1

Macbeth:
"Art thou but / A dagger of the mind, a false creation?"

Characters: Macbeth

Analysis: The thought of killing King Duncan is so disturbing that it is already starting to affect Macbeth's mind. The dagger is such a powerful hallucination that he questions his own senses and his ability to know whether it is real. The dagger could also have been conjured by the Witches in order to ensure that Macbeth goes ahead with killing the King. Macbeth asks the dagger if it is a 'false creation'; this metaphor could emphasise that instead of a true creation from God, it is a 'false creation' of evil. 'false' could also link to Macbeth's own deceit and untrustworthy actions.

Context: Macbeth is still deeply conflicted about killing King Duncan and hallucinates, seeing a dagger.

Themes: Appearance versus reality, guilt, loyalty, the supernatural, violence

Techniques: Metaphor, rhetorical question

Structure: A soliloquy in iambic pentameter, with irregularities

Using this quotation: This quotation can be used to demonstrate Macbeth's disturbed and conflicted thoughts and also to explore the role of the supernatural in the play.

Links in the text: This quotation links to later apparitions experienced by Macbeth, for example Banquo's Ghost.

Questions to consider:
- How does Shakespeare emphasise the moral difference between killing soldiers on the battlefield and murdering the King?

Quotation 12

Act 2, Scene 2

Macbeth:

"Will all great Neptune's ocean wash this blood / Clean from my hand? No, this my hand will rather / The multitudinous seas incarnadine, / Making the green one red."

Characters: Macbeth

Analysis: Macbeth would have had a large amount of blood on his hands after stabbing King Duncan. However, the blood is not just a physical representation of the murder, it is also a symbol of Macbeth's guilt and how that guilt will permanently stay with him. Macbeth asks if the Roman god Neptune would be able to wash the blood away with all the oceans of the world. Macbeth knows how awful his crime is and he appeals to a god, as the only being powerful enough to remove the evidence of his crime. Macbeth does not appeal to the Christian God as he has already confessed to Lady Macbeth that he cannot say 'amen'. In the absence of ability to appeal to a Christian God, he must instead appeal to a more ancient, or perhaps Pagan, one. Macbeth answers his own plea, confirming that it would be impossible to remove the stain of such an awful sin, instead all the seas will redden or 'incarnadine', 'making the green one red'.

Context: Macbeth has just murdered King Duncan and he is staring down at Duncan's blood on his hands.

The reference to turning water red is an allusion or reference to the Biblical story of the Ten Plagues of Egypt in Exodus, where Moses thrusts his staff into the Nile, turning the water red. In the story of Moses, the Pharaoh loses his first-born son in a plague sent by God as punishment for his cruelty and hatred.

Themes: Good and evil, guilt, treason, violence

Techniques: Biblical imagery, metaphor, rhetorical question

Structure: Iambic pentameter* with breaks – the final line is six syllables, missing four beats of the full rhythm. This pause could reflect Macbeth's despair, or perhaps he cuts himself short when Lady Macbeth re-enters.

Using this quotation: This quotation is essential for a question about Macbeth's transformation and for the theme of violence and good versus evil.

Links in the text: The use of blood as a symbol for guilt is present throughout the play; Lady Macbeth sees blood on her hands that she cannot remove in Act 5, Scene 1.

Questions to consider:
- How many references to blood can you think of throughout the play? Why is blood used as a motif by Shakespeare?

Quotation 13

Act 2, Scene 2

Lady Macbeth:
"My hands are of your colour; but I shame / To wear a heart so white."

Characters: Lady Macbeth, talking to Macbeth

Analysis: When Lady Macbeth says to Macbeth 'my hands are of your colour' she is referring to the blood covering both characters' hands. This quotation also means that Lady Macbeth is involved in the murder; she is now a direct part of it. Lady Macbeth insults or accuses Macbeth of being a coward, saying that she would 'shame' to 'wear a heart so white', referring to Macbeth's refusal to return to the scene of the murder. The adjective 'white' refers to Macbeth's 'surrender' or cowardly nature. The second line is only six beats, demonstrating a pause that could represent a moment of tension or shock from Macbeth. This is also another example of Lady Macbeth's emasculation of Macbeth as she attacks his lack of bravery. However, Shakespeare could be revealing flaws and weaknesses in Lady Macbeth's character. Although Lady Macbeth is involved in covering up the murder, she did not kill King Duncan, so it is not quite true that her involvement is the same as that of Macbeth. However, although the 'white heart' is supposed to be referring to Macbeth, it could also foreshadow Lady Macbeth's own guilt in later scenes.

Context: Having just murdered King Duncan, Macbeth has failed to carry out the next part of the plan, which is to put Duncan's blood on the guards and put their daggers beside them. Lady Macbeth must put the daggers back and put the blood on the guards herself. Lady Macbeth ends up with blood on her hands as Macbeth does, which later haunts her in Act 5.

Themes: Blood, guilt

Techniques: Blood imagery, foreshadowing, metaphor

Structure: Iambic pentameter

Using this quotation: This quotation is useful when answering questions on Lady Macbeth and the themes of guilt and blood imagery.

Links in the text: Compare Lady Macbeth's arrogance to her fragile nature in Act 5, Scene 1.

Questions to consider:
- How many other quotations about blood and its associations with guilt can you think of?

Quotation 14

Act 2, Scene 4

Old Man:
"'Tis unnatural…On Tuesday last, / A falcon, towering in her pride of place, / Was by a mousing owl hawk'd at and kill'd"

Characters: The 'Old Man', talking to Ross

Analysis: Shakespeare most likely intended for the 'falcon' in this extended metaphor* to be King Duncan. The King was second only to God in the chain of being and so was at the 'top of the food chain' in a sense, just as the falcon is. The 'mousing owl' is supposed to be the prey of the falcon, however the natural order has now been corrupted and the owl has killed the falcon. The 'mousing owl' symbolises Macbeth, who has corrupted the natural order by killing the King. This one act of going against the natural order is so severe, that it affects the wider balance of nature in Scotland itself.

Context: The murder of King Duncan has taken place and the world seems to have become darker and more corrupted afterwards. The Old Man, having lived 70 years, has not experienced a time as dark as this.

The Great Chain of Being* that is referenced in this scene is based on the early modern belief that God created an order of hierarchy.

At the top of the hierarchy was God, followed by the angels. On earth, the monarch was at the top, answering to God alone, followed by the rest of humanity. Your position in society was believed to be where God had chosen you to be. When Macbeth breaks the natural order of the world by murdering the King, nature became chaotic. This is linked to the divine right of kings – if the wrong person was on the throne, chaos would be created in the country, including nature.

Themes: Good and evil, nature

Techniques: Extended metaphor

Structure: Iambic pentameter

Using this quotation: This quotation can be used in a question on good and evil or a question on the importance of nature.

Links in the text: Bird imagery is very important in the play; the raven that Lady Macbeth names.

Questions to consider:
- Why has Shakespeare included this scene in the play?

Quotation 15

Act 3, Scene 1

Banquo:
"I fear, / Thou play'dst most foully for't:"

Characters: Banquo, talking about Macbeth

Analysis: At the start of the play, Banquo is both Macbeth's brother in arms and closest friend. Banquo 'fears' that his friend has committed murder, that he has lost Macbeth, and that maybe his murder is next. The verb 'play'dst' emphasises that Banquo believes this murder to be planned and prepared in a Machiavellian way. The 'most foully for't' is a metaphor for treason, the worst, or most foul, crime possible. It is almost as though Banquo cannot openly express the idea that Macbeth murdered the King; it is too awful to say aloud. Perhaps Banquo also realises that part of him would be capable of the same act, as Macbeth and Banquo are very similar in many ways.

Context: Banquo is privately voicing his suspicions that Macbeth is somehow behind the murder of King Duncan; as the only other person to meet the Witches, Banquo not only knows what they said to Macbeth, but how captivated Macbeth was by them.

Niccolò di Bernardo dei Machiavelli (1469-1527) was particularly interested in political philosophy and the term 'Machiavellian' became popular following his treatise *The Prince*. The text was infamous due to claims that it recommended that politicians should act immorally, for example being deceitful or murdering innocent people, to keep their power. Macbeth's ambition and desire for power, combined with his methods of gaining the throne, have many similarities with the concept of the Machiavellian politician or prince.

Themes: Ambition, good and evil, treason

Techniques: Alliteration, metaphor

Structure: Iambic pentameter

Using this quotation: This quotation is central to a question on Banquo and the relationship between Banquo and Macbeth.

Links in the text: This scene compares with Banquo and Macbeth's initial encounter with the Witches and the different reactions that they have.

Questions to consider:
- How does Shakespeare portray the changing relationship between Macbeth and Banquo?

Quotation 16

Act 3, Scene 2

Macbeth:
"O, full of scorpions is my mind, dear wife!"

Characters: Macbeth, talking to Lady Macbeth

Analysis: Macbeth has planned the murder of Banquo without the involvement of Lady Macbeth. Lady Macbeth attempts to calm Macbeth and involve herself in the plan to murder Banquo. Macbeth reacts aggressively to Lady Macbeth's attempts to control him. Macbeth's use of the word 'scorpions' to describe his thoughts has several meanings. The metaphor of the 'scorpions' describes the deadly nature of Macbeth's thoughts; they are lethal and murderous. Furthermore, the image of scorpions crawling around in Macbeth's brain implies that the thoughts are painful to him as well, perhaps as the last elements of his conscience. Moreover, scorpions are 'evil' creatures, symbolising evil thoughts. The scorpion is also an exotic creature, perhaps conveying the idea that thoughts of killing Banquo would have previously been alien to Macbeth. Macbeth is also very pointedly stating to his wife that his mind is full of violent thoughts and this could be interpreted as a threat towards Lady Macbeth.

Context: Macbeth's paranoid thoughts are increasing, and he has already instructed murderers to kill Banquo.

Themes: Ambition, good and evil, violence

Techniques: Metaphor*

Structure: Iambic pentameter

Using this quotation: This quotation can be used for questions on Macbeth, Lady Macbeth and their relationship. This quotation is also excellent for discussions of violence and ambition.

Links in the text: This quotation demonstrates a shift in power in Macbeth and Lady Macbeth's relationship. Earlier in the play, Lady Macbeth plans the details of Duncan's murder and manipulates Macbeth when he has doubts. By Act 3, Scene 2, the roles have reversed; Macbeth drives the plans for Banquo's murder and intimidates Lady Macbeth when she tries to take control.

Questions to consider:
- How has Shakespeare conveyed the change in the relationship between Macbeth and Lady Macbeth?

Quotation 17

Act 3, Scene 4

Macbeth:
"Thou canst not say I did it: never shake / Thy gory locks at me"

Characters: Macbeth, talking to Banquo's ghost

Analysis: Macbeth is deeply shaken by the appearance of the Ghost of Banquo at the banquet. Macbeth tries to confront the ghost, stating that the ghost cannot say Macbeth killed him. Macbeth then sees the ghost shaking his head at him and tries to command him to stop, ordering him to stop shaking his 'gory locks'. Banquo has 'gory locks' or bloody hair, as he was struck many times over the head. Banquo is most likely shaking his head in disgust at Macbeth's actions. Banquo could also be warning Macbeth to not go after his son Fleance, who managed to escape the ambush. It is also possible that the ghost is not a supernatural* being or apparition but is actually a hallucination caused by Macbeth's guilt. Macbeth has just been told Banquo has been murdered and has also been told the state of Banquo's corpse. It would not be difficult for Macbeth's mind to create an image of Banquo in this state. Finally, it could be argued that Banquo's appearance is an allusion to Christ: Banquo's head is bloody as

Christ's was from the crown of thorns, and Banquo reappears after death.

Context: After the murderers tell Macbeth that Banquo has been violently killed, Macbeth sees the Ghost of Banquo, although no other characters in the scene can see the ghost.

Themes: Guilt, the supernatural, violence

Techniques: Metaphor, violent imagery

Structure: Iambic pentameter

Using this quotation: This quotation can be used for Macbeth's transformation, a question on Banquo, or the themes of guilt and the supernatural.

Links in the text: Consider the other spirits that Macbeth sees throughout the play and what function they have. For example, in Act 3, Scene 4 Lady Macbeth states to Macbeth: "This is the very painting of your fear / This is the air-drawn dagger which you said / Led you to Duncan". Like with the Ghost of Banquo, the dagger is a symbol of Macbeth's mental instability and guilt.

Questions to consider:
- What is the significance of Macbeth's reaction to seeing the Ghost of Banquo?
- What is important about the public display of Macbeth's mental instability in front of his court? How does it link with the disrupted Great Chain of Being and divine right of kings?

Quotation 18

Act 4, Scene 1

Second Witch:

"By the pricking of my thumbs, / Something wicked this way comes."

Characters: Second Witch, describing Macbeth

Analysis: A Jacobean audience would have been aware of the superstition that a sudden sharp pain in the body would have signalled the potential arrival of evil. Shakespeare portrays the Witches as being very sensitive to the signals and sensations of approaching evil. The Second Witch senses evil through the 'pricking of her thumbs'; the use of the verb 'pricking' could imply that the Witch finds the sensation pleasurable. Macbeth is described as 'something wicked'; Shakespeare is illustrating Macbeth's ongoing transformation from a 'brave' and noble warrior to a violent dictator and mass murderer. Macbeth is not even a man, but a 'thing'. This mirrors Banquo's language to describe the Witches in Act 1, Scene 3, asking "What are these" and "Were such things here as we do speak about? / Or have we eaten on the insane root / That takes the reason prisoner?" Both the Second Witch and Banquo use dehumanising language, and ironically, the Witches' influence over Macbeth does indeed steal his 'reason' until he is a 'thing' incapable of thinking rationally, just as Banquo worried about at the beginning of the play.

Context: The Witches open Act 4 by brewing a powerful spell, listing many ingredients considered to be rare and evil. Macbeth's approach is sensed by the Witches as an evil being looming.

Themes: Good and evil, the supernatural, the Witches

Techniques: Metaphor, rhyme

Structure: Trochaic tetrameter which emphasises the supernatural nature of the Witch's sensation.

Using this quotation: This quotation can be used as part of Macbeth's character arc, or for a question on the Witches, or the importance of supernatural in the play.

Links in the text: Compare this meeting with Macbeth's first encounter with the Witches: how did Macbeth react to the Witches? How did the Witches react to Macbeth?

Questions to consider:
- How do the Witches feel about Macbeth's arrival at this point in the play?
- How has Shakespeare portrayed Macbeth's transformation until this point?

Quotation 19

Act 4, Scene 1

Second Apparition:

"Be bloody, bold, and resolute; laugh to scorn / The power of man, for none of woman born / Shall harm Macbeth."

Characters: Second apparition, summoned by the Witches, talking to Macbeth

Analysis: The first apparition, a helmeted head, has warned Macbeth about Macduff, the Thane of Fife. The second apparition, a 'bloody child', seems to contradict the first as it says: 'none of woman born / Shall harm Macbeth'. However, the second apparition's prophecy contains a trick, or loophole. The 'bloody child' represents Macduff, who was not 'born' of woman, but cut out or 'ripped' from his mother prematurely through a caesarean section. However, Macbeth does not know about Macduff's entrance into the world and takes the second prophecy as cancelling out the first. Macbeth takes the prophecy at face value, that he should be confident and consider himself invincible. Macbeth should be 'bloody, bold and resolute'; he should continue to be violent, brave and not surrender to his enemies. Macbeth should not fear his enemies but instead 'laugh' at the 'power of man'.

Context: Macbeth has gone to the Witches to demand more answers from them.

Themes: The Supernatural, fate

Techniques: List of three, alliteration

Structure: The final line of the prophecy is only four syllables, six short of the iambic pentameter. Firstly, this could be because Shakespeare was conveying the uniqueness of the apparition by allowing it to break the rhythm of the language; secondly, the apparition could be stopping short of revealing the 'loophole' in the prophecy; finally, it could convey Macbeth's shock at the idea of his own invincibility.

Using this quotation: This is a useful quotation in a discussion of the supernatural and its role within Macbeth. It can also be used to discuss the character development of Macbeth.

Links in the text: The third prophecy, like the second, contains a trick or loophole that gives Macbeth misplaced confidence in his own invulnerability. The prophecy states that Macbeth will not be beaten or 'vanquished' until 'Great Birnam wood to high Dunsinane hill / Shall come against him.' Macbeth understands the third prophecy as a metaphor for something impossible, that a wood will not move up the hill and attack him. However, as we find out at the end of the play, each soldier in the army that attacks Macbeth is ordered to carry a branch of a tree from Birnam Wood; as the army is huge, Birnam Wood is essentially cut down and carried up Dunsinane Hill in order to camouflage the numbers and formation of the army.

Questions to consider:
- Why do the Witches reveal these prophecies to Macbeth?

Quotation 20

Act 4, Scene 3

Macduff:

"He has no children. All my pretty ones? / Did you say all? O hell-kite! All? / What, all my pretty chickens and their dam / At one fell swoop?"

Characters: Macduff, talking about Macbeth

Analysis: Macduff is in shock at the brutal killing of his family. Macduff struggles to accept that all his loved ones have been killed at once and the repetition of 'All?' emphasises this. Macduff's shock is also conveyed by his inability to name his wife and children, instead calling them 'my pretty ones' and 'my pretty chickens and their dam'. The metaphor 'chickens and their dam' emphasises how helpless and vulnerable Macduff's family were and how they were innocent victims; chickens are defenceless, domesticated* creatures who cannot fight back. The use of 'chickens and their dam' – dam meaning mother hen – could also suggest Macduff's guilt; Macduff left his family vulnerable to attack by travelling to England to meet Malcolm. Macduff calls Macbeth a 'hell-kite'; a bird of prey from hell itself. Macbeth has 'swooped' down and killed the whole of Macduff's family at once. The only way that Macduff can understand how Macbeth could have done this is that 'he has no children', but Macduff still struggles to comprehend* what Macbeth has done.

Context: Macduff has just been told that his wife and children have been killed at his castle home in Fife.

Themes: Good and evil, guilt, violence

Techniques: Bird imagery, extended metaphor, repetition

Structure: Iambic pentameter – the final line is only four syllables, which is completed by Malcolm, to bring Macduff out of his shock and bring control to the situation.

Using this quotation: This quotation is key in a question about Macduff and can also be used to demonstrate Macbeth's violence.

Links in the text: This quotation links to Macduff's quest for revenge in the final Act of the play. The imagery also links to other descriptions of Macbeth as a bird, or as an agent of Hell.

Questions to consider:
- How does Shakespeare use Hell imagery and animal imagery to describe Macbeth?

Quotation 21

Act 5, Scene 1

Lady Macbeth:
"Out, damned spot! out, I say! - One: two: why, / then, 'tis time to do't. - Hell is murky!"

Characters: Lady Macbeth

Analysis: Lady Macbeth has become overwhelmed by guilt; she has been driven mad by it. Shakespeare presents Lady Macbeth's guilt as a metaphorical 'spot' of blood that she is convinced is still on her hand and that will not be washed off. Lady Macbeth feels guilty primarily for her part in the murder of Duncan, but she also feels at least partly responsible for the murders that Macbeth goes on to commit. Shakespeare illustrates Lady Macbeth's guilt at the murder of Duncan, Banquo and Macduff's family by having her reference them in a broken and disordered way throughout the scene. Lady Macbeth tries to command the 'spot' to leave, perhaps as she commanded Macbeth, but she is unsuccessful. Lady Macbeth then relives the moments before King Duncan's murder, counting 'one, two'; perhaps the bell that signalled Macbeth to go ahead. Lady Macbeth then seems to stare into Hell itself, saying it is 'murky'. She also has a very real fear of damnation or going to Hell, referring as she does to the 'damned spot'. The 'damned spot' could also be a reference to the Biblical story of Cain, who was marked by God for murdering his brother.

Context: A doctor has been called by Lady Macbeth's 'gentlewoman' or nurse maid as Lady Macbeth has been sleepwalking and saying shocking things.

Themes: Ambition, blood, good and evil, guilt, Hell, justice, treason

Techniques: Blood imagery, imagery of Hell, metaphor, repetition

Structure: Broken or fractured prose

Using this quotation: This quotation is vital when discussing Lady Macbeth, blood, ambition, guilt and good and evil. This scene illustrates that Lady Macbeth has failed in her attempt to remain free from guilt in her pursuit of power and instead the guilt has overwhelmed her. This quotation links in with the use of blood imagery throughout the play and shows the harsh consequences* of committing treason.

Links in the text: This scene could be linked and contrasted with Act 1, Scene 5. In Act 1, Scene 5, Lady Macbeth is powerful, arrogant and ambitious. Shakespeare has Lady Macbeth speak in blank verse and she calls to the spirits to remove anything maternal from her body and to cut off the path to her conscience. Act 5, Scene 1 stands in stark contrast, as Lady Macbeth speaks in broken prose, fearful of Hell and unwittingly confessing her sins.

Questions to consider:
- How does Shakespeare portray Lady Macbeth's transformation from Act 1, Scene 5 to Act 5, Scene 1?

Quotation 22

Act 5, Scene 1

Lady Macbeth:
"Here's the smell of the blood still: all the / perfumes of Arabia will not sweeten this little / hand. Oh, oh, oh!"

Characters: Lady Macbeth

Analysis: Lady Macbeth not only imagines that she can see the blood on her hands, she can also smell it; this may be because she is sleeping, or because of how overwhelming her guilt is. Lady Macbeth is either rubbing or washing her hands repeatedly, but the metaphorical blood will not disappear, and the smell remains 'still'. Lady Macbeth knows the blood will never leave her, because the guilt will not. Even perfume from Arabia, known for its aromatic spices and scents, could not mask the smell. The verb 'sweeten' refers to masking or removing the smell of blood, but it could also refer to Lady Macbeth failing to restore her femininity. Lady Macbeth helped plan a murder and was involved in the cover up; there is no 'sweetening' of her hand or her womanhood. The repetition of 'oh' signifies complete despair, a complete breakdown and surrender from Lady Macbeth. Following her manipulation and insulting accusations of Macbeth being 'brainsickly', 'too full o' th' milk of human kindness' and 'infirm of purpose' when he raised doubts about the murder of King Duncan, Lady Macbeth's breakdown is deeply ironic given that she ends her life in deep guilt and misery.

Context: Lady Macbeth is sleepwalking in this scene and the guilt she feels at the murders has deeply disturbed her.

Themes: Blood, guilt, violence

Techniques: Irony, metaphor, repetition, sensory imagery

Structure: Broken prose

Using this quotation: This quotation can be used in a question about Lady Macbeth's transformation and questions on the theme of guilt and blood.

Links in the text: This quotation can be compared to Macbeth's plea to Neptune in Act 2, Scene 2.

Questions to consider:
- How can Macbeth's plea be considered masculine and Lady Macbeth's feminine?

Quotation 23

Act 5, Scene 8

Macduff:
"Turn, hell-hound, turn!"

Characters: Macduff, commanding Macbeth

Analysis: By this point, almost everyone is afraid of Macbeth; he was an impressive warrior when the play began but he is now a murderous dictator. Macduff therefore shows great bravery in challenging Macbeth in the way that he does. Macduff uses the metaphor 'hell hound' to refer to Macbeth. A hell hound would guard the boundary or entrance to the underworld or Hell. Macduff is calling Macbeth a symbol or harbinger of death. Furthermore, calling Macbeth a 'hound' rather than a man is insulting, as a 'hound' is less than a man. The repetition of 'turn' emphasises the power of Macduff's command; he expects and demands to be obeyed and for Macbeth to fight him.

Context: It is the final battle of the play and Macduff has finally found Macbeth; Macduff challenges Macbeth in order to get revenge for the murder of his family.

Themes: Good and evil, justice

Techniques: Metaphor, repetition

Structure: Iambic pentameter – the quotation is only four beats, leaving it six beats short of the iambic pentameter; this could be Shakespeare instructing the actor playing Macbeth to perhaps turn slowly or stare silently at Macduff, increasing the tension and sense of menace.

Using this quotation: This quotation would be central to a question on Macduff and could also be used in a discussion of Macbeth, as it is a description of Macbeth by another character. The themes of good and evil and justice are important here, as Macduff is seeking revenge for his family.

Links in the text: When Macduff first hears that Macbeth has murdered his family, Macduff calls him a 'hell kite', a bird of prey from Hell that has killed his family 'at one fell swoop'. Consider also when Macbeth insults the manhood of the murderers by saying that if they were dogs, they would be in the lowest category, just as they are in the lowest category of men.

Questions to consider:
- What other imagery is used to describe Macbeth in the final scenes of the play?

Quotation 24

Act 5, Scene 8

Macduff:

"Despair thy charm; / And let the angel whom thou still hast served / Tell thee, Macduff was from his mother's womb / Untimely ripp'd."

Characters: Macduff, talking to Macbeth

Analysis: Macduff tells Macbeth to 'despair thy charm'; the prophecy from the Witches is worthless. It is interesting that Macduff refers to the 'angel' that Macbeth serves; this is most likely in reference to the story of Lucifer, the devil, who was originally one of God's highest angels before being cast out for defiance. Macduff is telling Macbeth that he has been tricked; that the 'angel' (Lucifer) knew all along that Macduff was not 'born of woman' in the natural way but was instead born through what we would now call a caesarean section. However, as opposed to the modern operation performed today, Macduff was 'untimely ripped'. This phrase suggests that Macduff's mother was dying, and Macduff was delivered early and violently in order to stop him dying along with his mother.

Context: Macbeth believes himself to be protected by the Witches' prophecy that 'no man of woman born' can kill him. Macbeth tells Macduff about the prophecy to get Macduff to give up. Macduff replies that he was not born naturally.

Themes: The supernatural, violence

Techniques: Biblical reference, metaphor

Structure: Iambic pentameter – the final line is only four syllables, which emphasises the early and violent ending of Macduff's mother's pregnancy, and Macbeth's shocked silence that he has been tricked and can be killed.

Using this quotation: This quotation is useful when discussing the importance of Macduff and the Witches' manipulation of Macbeth. It can also be used when discussing Macbeth's ignorance and willing acceptance of the preternatural.

Links in the text: Think about how each of the prophecies in Act 4, Scene 1 were cleverly disguised tricks and how each of them ended up having a loophole.

Questions to consider:
- Why did the Witches trick Macbeth? What were Shakespeare's possible intentions?

Quotation 25

Act 5, Scene 8

Malcolm:
"Of this dead butcher and his fiend-like queen"

Characters: Malcolm, talking about Macbeth and Lady Macbeth

Analysis: Macbeth's transformation from brave and noble warrior to defeated violent dictator is complete. The metaphor 'butcher' conveys Macbeth's violent and bloody nature and the senseless killing of so many. Furthermore, not using Macbeth's name, simply 'butcher', further illustrates the contempt that Malcolm has for Macbeth, and that Macbeth will forever be remembered in this way. Lady Macbeth is described as a 'fiend-like' demon that influenced Macbeth's descent into bloody violence. Interestingly, Malcolm calls Lady Macbeth a 'queen'; this may be because Shakespeare is placing Lady Macbeth in a final, dominant position in the relationship. This is hardly flattering however, as it almost seems to place more blame on Lady Macbeth as the person controlling Macbeth, who was simply a 'butcher', obeying orders.

Context: Macbeth has been defeated and Malcolm has been officially recognised as the new King of Scotland. This re-establishes the divine right of kings.

Themes: Ambition, blood, kingship, treason, violence

Techniques: Imagery of Hell, metaphor

Structure: Iambic pentameter. The cyclical structure of traitorous betrayal is complete at the end of the play as Macbeth is executed, like the traitorous Thane of Cawdor he executes at the beginning of the play. This scene also fulfils the Greek tragedy concept of nemesis – named after the Greek goddess of revenge – as Macbeth is justly punished for his hubris and evil deeds.

Using this quotation: This is an excellent quotation to use for a variety of questions. This quotation marks the end of Macbeth's and Lady Macbeth's arc in the text and is also a final comment on their relationship. This quotation can also be used for the themes of violence, ambition and kingship, as at this point Malcolm has been made king.

Links in the text: This quotation links back to Shakespeare's first description of Macbeth in the Sergeant's speech in Act 1, Scene 2. Macbeth 'carved out his passage' and 'unseamed' the traitor 'from the nave to the chaps', as though he were using butchery skills.

Questions to consider:
- How has Shakespeare shown the transformation from 'brave Macbeth' to 'dead butcher' throughout the play?
- Why does Shakespeare have Malcolm call Lady Macbeth 'queen'?

Glossary of Key Terms

Ambition: A strong desire to do or achieve something.

Alliteration: When words that start with the same or similar sound are used repeatedly in a phrase or sentence.

Appropriate: Fitting the practical or social requirements of the situation; seemly; suitable.

Atmosphere: A mood or tone that is found within a place or among a group.

Biblical: Relating to or contained in the Bible.

Character arc: The changes a character goes through over the course of a text. If a story has a character arc, the character begins as one sort of person and gradually changes in response to developments in the story.

Commission: An order granting authority to perform a certain task or function.

Composed: To create music or written works. *I need silence while I'm composing.*

Comprehend: To understand or grasp the meaning of.

Consequence: That which follows; result.

Context: The circumstances in which something is done.

Crucial: Of decisive importance; critical.

Divine right of kings: The belief that kings derive their authority from God and not the people. God places monarchs in their roles and to murder a king is a terrible sin against God.

Domesticated: (Of an animal) tame and kept as a pet or on a farm.

Elizabethan: Elizabethan literature refers to bodies of work produced during the reign of Queen Elizabeth I (1558–1603).

Emasculation: Taking a man's sense of masculinity or identity.

Euphemism: A mild or indirect word or expression said instead of one considered to be too harsh or blunt when referring to something unpleasant or embarrassing.

Extended metaphor: A metaphor that is developed over several moments within a text; this can be in one scene or in several scenes.

Foiled: Prevented from happening or succeeding.

Great Chain of Being: The status of all different forms of life decided by God.

Iambic pentameter: A line with ten syllables organised into five pairs or 'metrical feet'. The first syllable in the pair will be unstressed, the second syllable will be stressed (i AM).

Irony or ironic: Something that is unexpected, often in an amusing way.

Jacobean: Jacobean literature, body of works written during the reign of James I of England (1603–25).

Juxtaposition: Placing two things close together or side by side. This is often done in order to show contrast, unlikeness or differences.

Metaphor: A phrase or image that is used to make a strong comparison between two things that are not alike but do have something in common.

Personification: Giving an animal or object qualities or abilities that only a human can have.

Preternatural: Things not seen to be normal, natural or Godly, such as the demonic and the deception and trickery of witches.

Repetition: Repeating a key word or phrase within a sentence or passage.

Rhetorical question: A question that is asked to make a point rather than for an answer.

Simile: A phrase or image that is used to make a comparison between two things, using the words 'like' or 'as'.

Soliloquy: When a character speaks their thoughts aloud on stage in verse when they are alone or if they believe themselves to be alone.

Succession to the throne: The rules for who should be next in line to the throne.

Supernatural: A force or being that exists outside of the laws of nature or science.

Thane: A person, ranking with an earl's son, holding lands of the King; the chief of a clan, who became one of the King's barons.

Trochaic tetrameter: A line of eight syllables organised in four pairs or 'trochaic feet'. A pair of syllables or 'trochee' has a stressed syllable, followed by an unstressed one.

Our fabulous new revision guides are out now!

25 Key Quotations for GCSE

- Romeo and Juliet
- A Christmas Carol
- Macbeth
- Dr Jekyll and Mr Hyde
- An Inspector Calls

GCSE Revision Guides

- An Inspector Calls
- A Christmas Carol
- Macbeth
- English Language

But that's not all! We've also got a host of annotation-friendly editions, containing oodles of space for you to fill with those all-important notes:

Annotation-Friendly Editions

- Dr Jekyll and Mr Hyde
- A Christmas Carol
- Romeo and Juliet
- Macbeth

… and lots more!

Available through Amazon, Waterstones, and all good bookshops!

About the author of this guide

Daniel Smith has been an English teacher for eight years and is currently the Second in English at Reigate School, an Outstanding Secondary School in Surrey. Mr Smith studied English Literature at Queens University Belfast before studying for his PGCE at Leeds University. With the English Language and Literature GCSEs moving to examinations only, Mr Smith recognised the importance of memorising key themes and quotations. The quotations and analysis in this guide are a result of discussions with colleagues and students in order to prepare for the demands of the English Literature GCSE.

About the editor of this guide

Hannah Rabey is Head of English at a school in Oxfordshire. Hannah studied Literature and History at the University of East Anglia before studying for her PGCE at the University of Oxford. Hannah is a GCSE examiner and is experienced with teaching all of the texts in the 25 Key Quotations revision guide series.

Printed in Great Britain
by Amazon